Fireflies

Edited by Heather C. Hudak

Published by Weigl Publishers Inc.
350 5th Avenue, Suite 3304, PMB 6G
New York, NY 10118-0069
Website: www.weigl.com

Library of Congress Cataloging-in-Publication Data

Fireflies : world of wonder / edited by Heather C. Hudak.
       p. cm.
 Includes index.
 ISBN 978-1-59036-868-8 (hard cover : alk. paper) -- ISBN 978-1-59036-869-5 (soft cover : alk. paper)
 1. Fireflies--Juvenile literature. I. Hudak, Heather C., 1975-
 QL596.L28F57 2009
 595.76'44--dc22

                          2008023852

Printed in the United States of America
1 2 3 4 5 6 7 8 9 0 12 11 10 09 08

Editor: Heather C. Hudak
Design: Terry Paulhus

Photo credits: Getty Images: 5, 8, 13, 17, 19, 21; © Phil Degginger/Alamy: cover, page 15.

All of the Internet URLs given in the book were valid at the time of publication. However, due to the dynamic nature of
the Internet, some addresses may have changed, or sites may have ceased to exist since publication. While the author
and publisher regret any inconvenience this may cause readers, no responsibility for any such changes can be accepted
by either the author or the publisher.

Every reasonable effort has been made to trace ownership and to obtain permission to reprint copyright material. The
publishers would be pleased to have any errors or omissions brought to their attention so that they may be corrected
in subsequent printings.

CONTENTS

What is a Firefly?

Have you ever wondered about the small creatures that light up the night during summer? These creatures are called fireflies.

A firefly is an insect. There are more than 2,000 types of firefly in the world.

Fireflies are beetles. These are insects with hard covers over their wings.

6

Back in Time

Fireflies are a part of an insect family called *Coleoptera*. The first coleoptera lived 275 million years ago. This was when dinosaurs roamed Earth.

Can you imagine having the biggest family in the world? Coleoptera are the largest insect family. They make up 25 percent of all living things.

Firefly Life Cycle

Female fireflies lay glowing eggs in the soil. They lay between 500 and 1,000 eggs at one time. The eggs hatch into **larvae** about four weeks later. The larvae also glow.

The larvae spend the summer eating. In winter, they live in small tunnels under the ground. Once the soil warms in spring, the larvae come out to eat. Then, they become **pupae**. The pupae grow for one to two-and-a-half weeks. Then, they turn into fireflies.

What Does a Firefly Look Like?

How many parts are on your body? A firefly has three main parts. These are the head, thorax, and abdomen. Most fireflies are black, with two red spots on their head.
Their outside shell is lined in yellow.

Fireflies have a hard shell, or **exoskeleton**. They have six legs that are joined to their thorax. Two **antennae** and **compound eyes** are found on their head.

Fireflies are up to 1 inch (2.5 centimeters) long. This is the same size as a paper clip.

head

thorax

abdomen

11

The Glow

Imagine if you could glow to attract friends and family! At night, the abdomen of the firefly glows a bright yellow-green color. A single firefly is almost as bright as half the glow of a candle.

Fireflies flash their light on and off to attract other fireflies.

A firefly's glow can barely be seen in daylight.

Have Wings, Will Fly!

How fast can you move when you carry a heavy bag? Fireflies do not fly fast because their lanterns are heavy and their wings are not very big.

Fireflies are the only glowing insects that have wings. Two tough outer wings protect the softer underwings and the body. Fireflies use their outer wings for balance during flight. The underwings are used to fly.

What's for Dinner?

When you were a baby, what did you eat? Firefly larvae have a special way of eating. Larvae stun their **prey**. Then, they inject it with a liquid that stops the prey from moving.

Fireflies eat only at night. This is when they are most active.

Some adult fireflies do not eat at all. Others eat plant **pollen** and insects.

Home Sweet Home

The best places to find fireflies are in meadows, lawns, woods, and streams. Fireflies live in warm climates all over the world.

During the day, fireflies hide in grass. This helps keep them safe from **predators**.

Insect Lore

The ancient **Mayans** linked fireflies with stars and their gods.

In China and Japan, students who could not afford electricity would read by the light of a firefly.

Make a Firefly

Supplies
Wooden ice-cream spoons, glow-in-the-dark paint, black paper, tissue or wax paper, glue

1. Use the wooden spoons that come with ice-cream cups as the body of the firefly.

2. Use glow-in-the-dark paint to color the wooden spoon. Wait for the paint to dry.

3. Cut two small circles out of the black paper. These will be the firefly's eyes. Glue the eyes on one end of the painted spoon.

4. To make wings, cut out two ovals from the tissue or wax paper. Next, glue on the wings. Be sure to place one on each side of the wooden spoon.

5. Switch off the lights. Does your firefly glow brightly in the dark?

Find Out More

To find out more about fireflies, visit these websites.

The Firefly Files
http://iris.biosci.ohio-state.
edu/projects/FFiles/
frfact.html

Firefly or Lightning Bug
www.enchantedlearning.
com/subjects/insects/
beetles/Fireflyprintout

Firefly information
www.essortment.com/
all/fireflyinformat_raql.html

FEATURE SITE:
http://animals.national
geographic.com/animals
/bugs/firefly.html

Glossary

antennae: long, slim feelers found on the head

compound eyes: eyes that are made up of many small visual units

exoskeleton: hard outer covering of the body

larvae: young insects

Mayans: Aboriginal Peoples that lived in Central and South America

pollen: a yellow powder produced by flowers

predators: animals that hunt other animals for food

prey: animals that are hunted for food

pupae: a stage between larvae and adult

Index